W9-AHS-245

HOUGHTON MIFFLIN

Reading

A Legacy of Literacy

Look at Us!

We Go to School

by Susan Gorman-Howe

illustrated by Maryann Cocca-Leffler

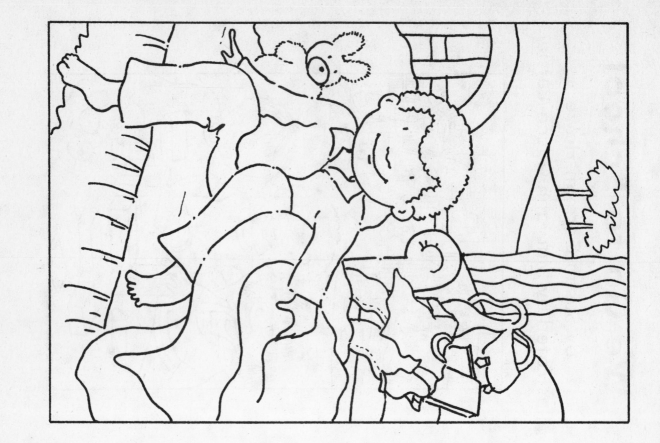

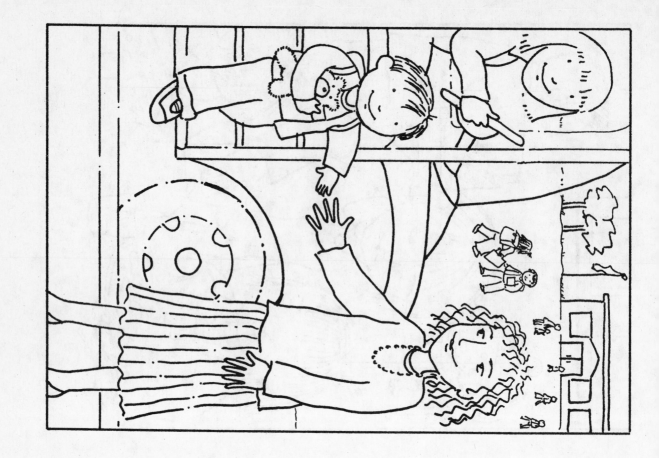

See What We Can Do

by Susan Gorman-Howe

illustrated by Sue Dennen

7A

Theme 1/Selection 2

8A

We Can Make It

by Susan Gorman-Howe

illustrated by Anthony Lewis

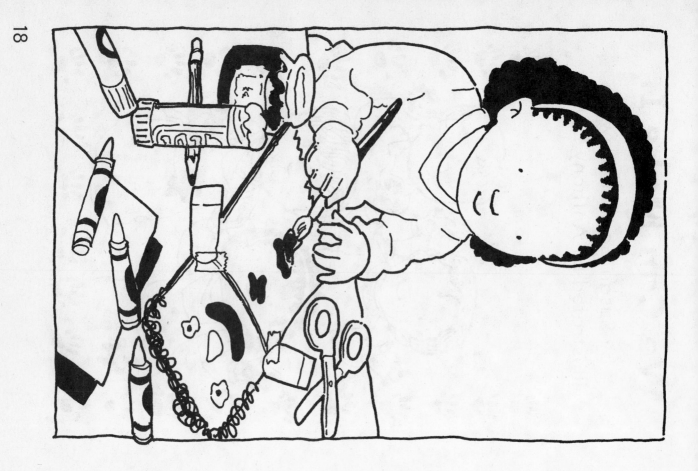

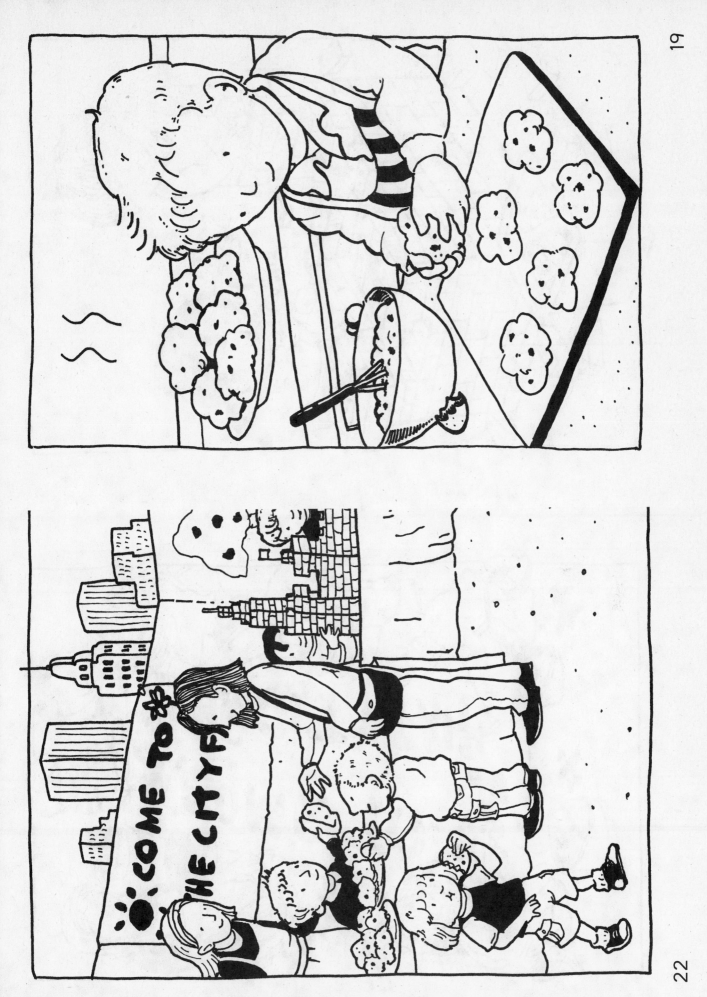

11A

Theme 1/Selection 3

HOUGHTON MIFFLIN
Reading
A Legacy of Literacy

Colors All Around

My Red Boat

by Susan Gorman-Howe

illustrated by Lauren Scheuer

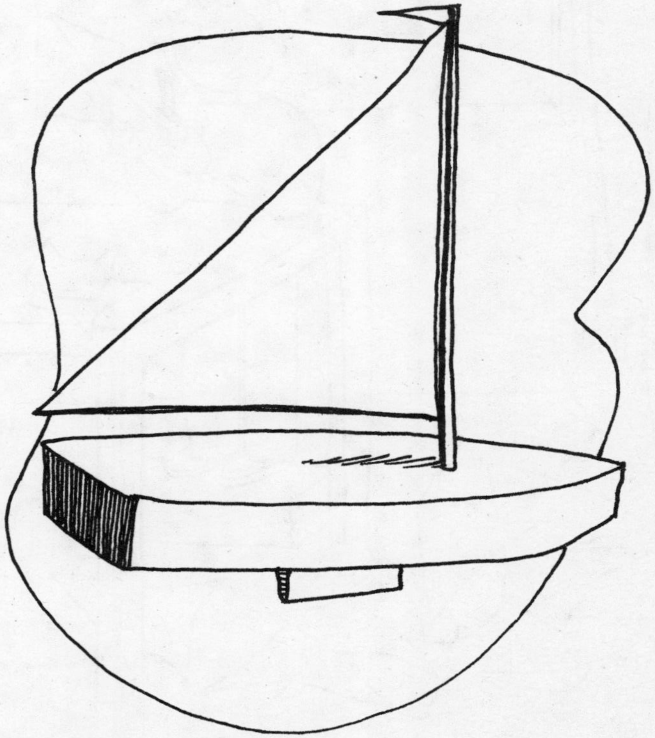

Theme 2/Selection 1

Theme 2/Selection 1

4B

Look at Me!

by Susan Gorman-Howe

illustrated by Jennifer Plecas

FACE PAINTING

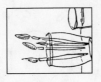

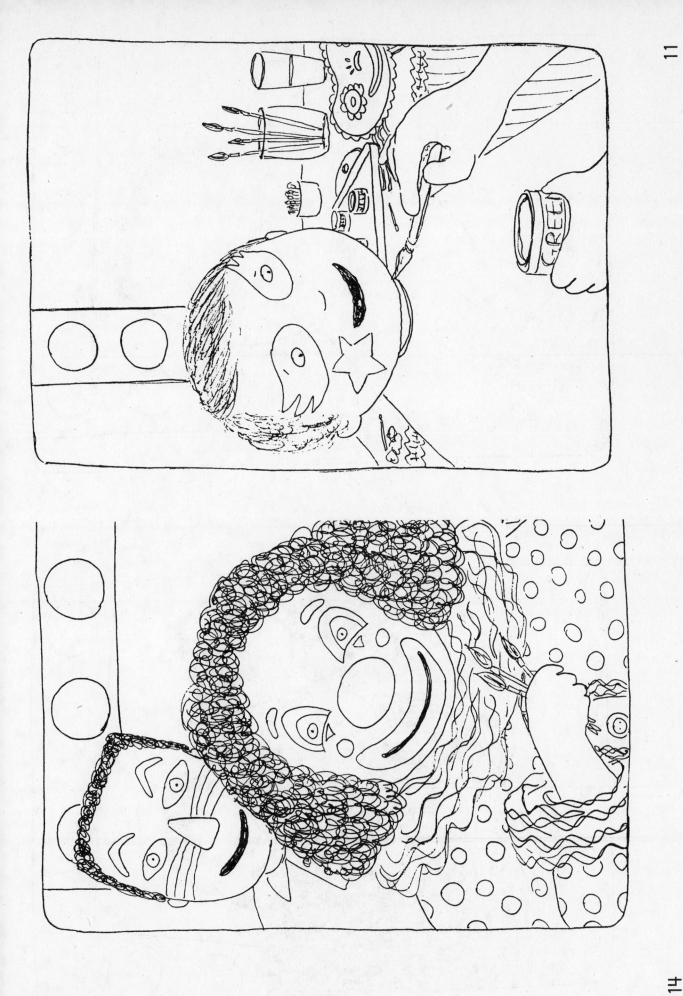

Theme 2/Selection 2

7B

Theme 2/Selection 2

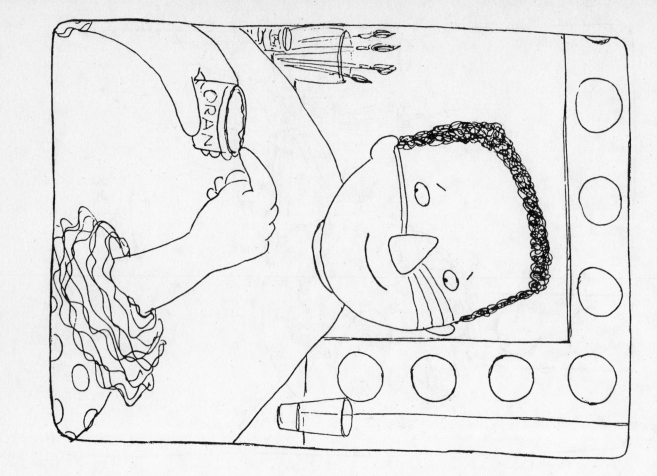

The Parade

by Susan Gorman-Howe
illustrated by Joan Paley

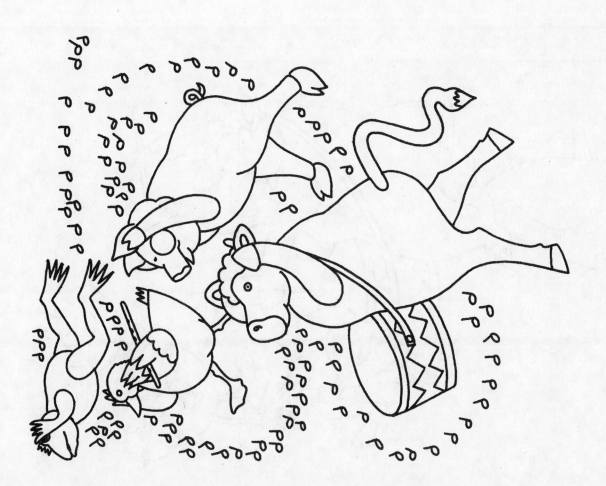

11B

Theme 2/Selection 3

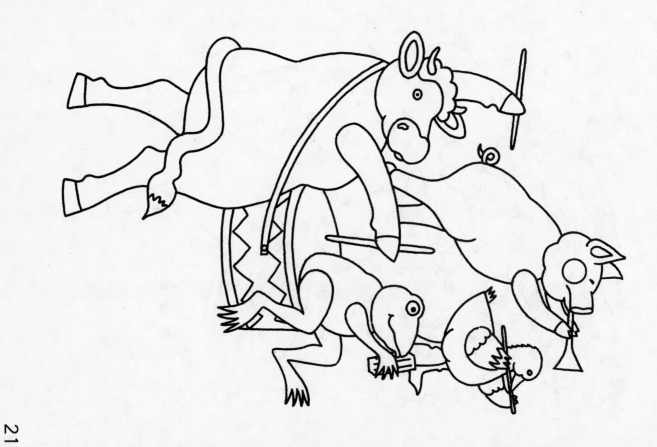

HOUGHTON MIFFLIN

Reading

A Legacy of Literacy

We're a Family

The Birthday Party

by Susan Gorman-Howe
illustrated by Grace Lin

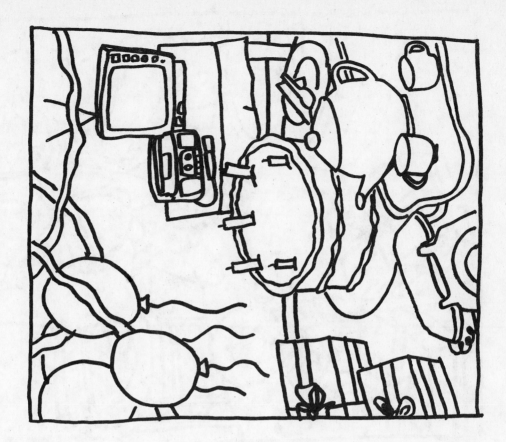

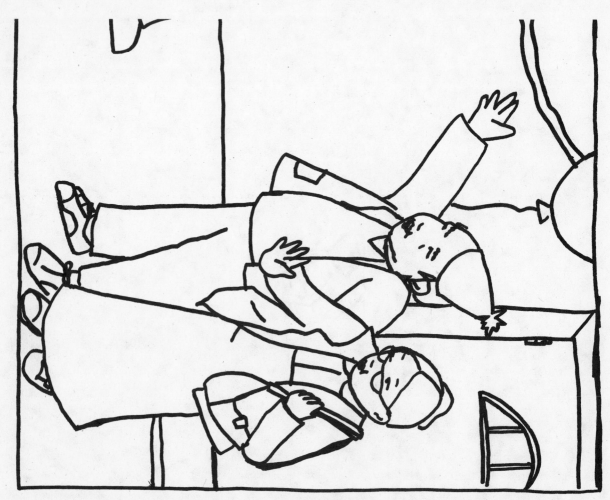

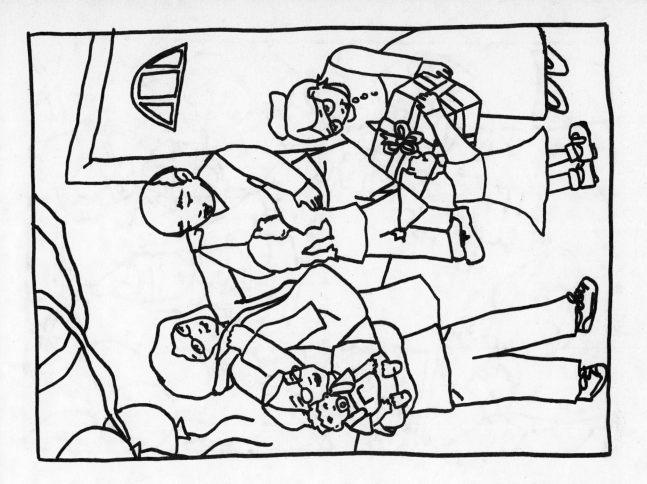

Theme 3/Selection 1

Theme 3/Selection 1

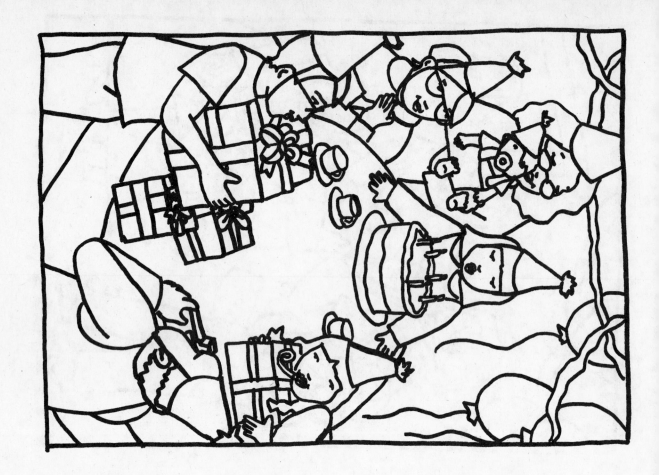

Baby Bear's Family

by Susan Gorman-Howe

illustrated by Angela Jarecki

9

Theme 3/Selection 2

7C

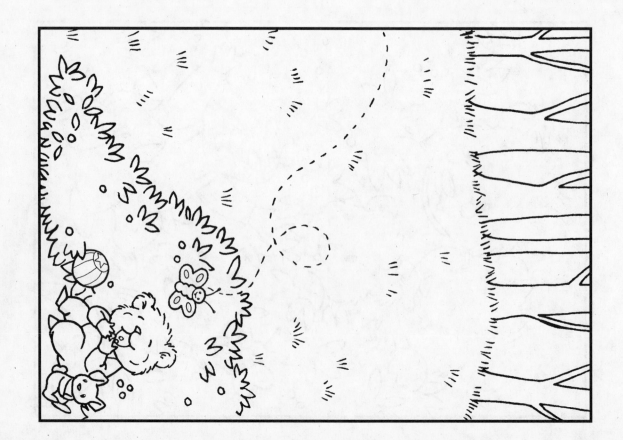

Cat's Surprise

by Susan Gorman-Howe
illustrated by Valeri Gorbachev

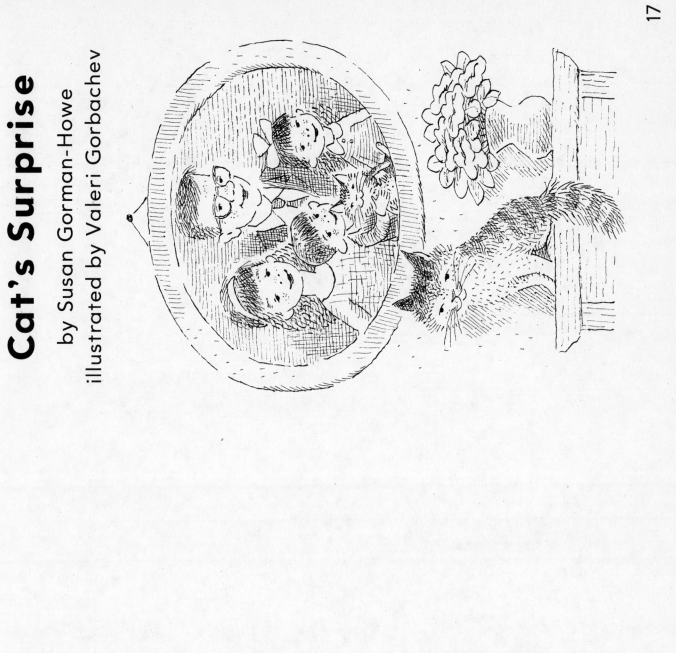

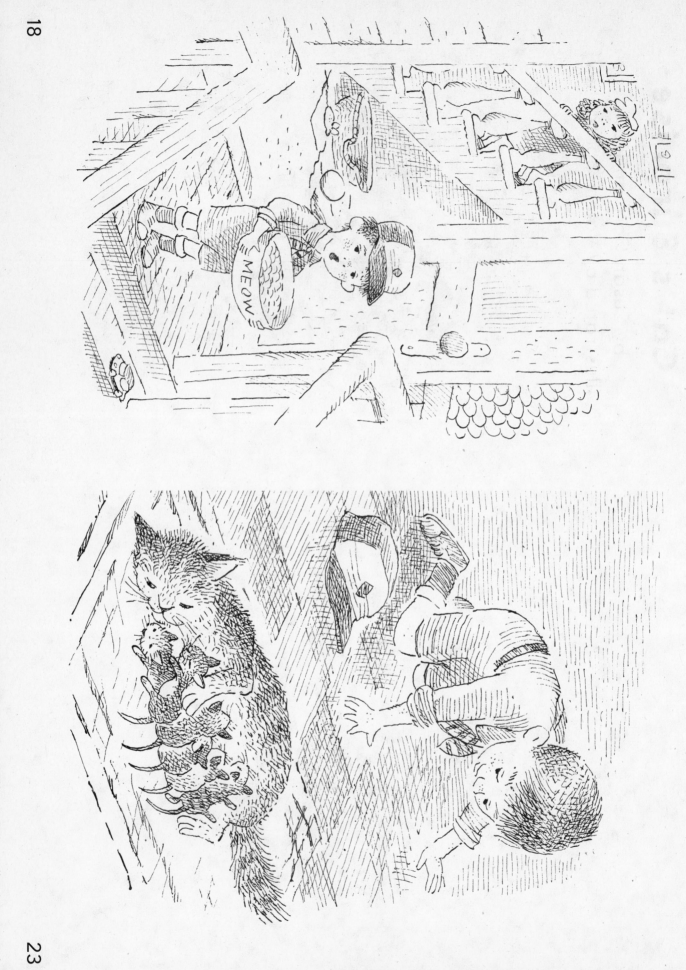

11C

Theme 3/Selection 3

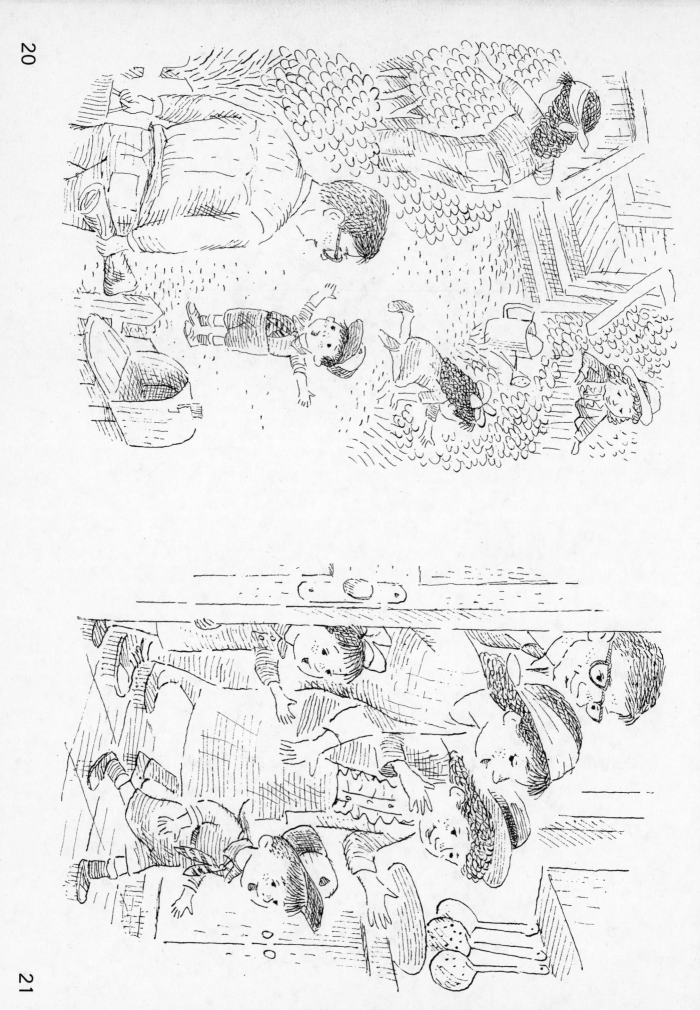

12C

HOUGHTON MIFFLIN

Reading

A Legacy of Literacy

Friends Together

Nat at Bat

by Elizabeth Kiley

illustrated by Holly Berry

1D

Bat, Nat!

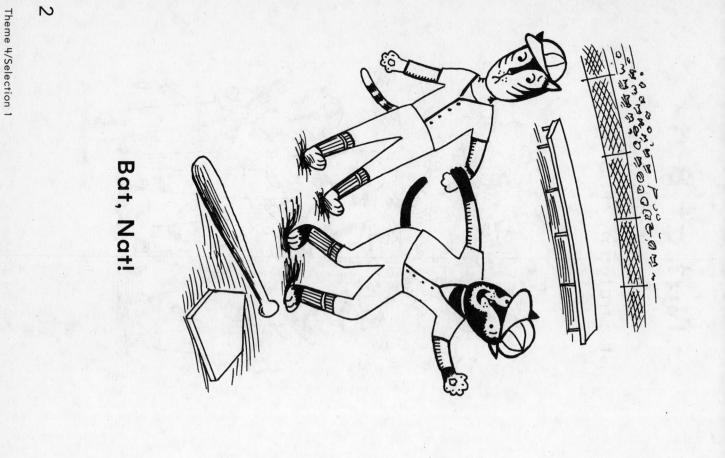

Nat sat.
My hat!

Theme 4/Selection 1

Theme 4/Selection 1

Bat, bat, bat, Nat!

Nat sat, sat, sat.

See Nat at bat!

A Vat

by Elizabeth Kiley

illustrated by Bob Kolar

mat

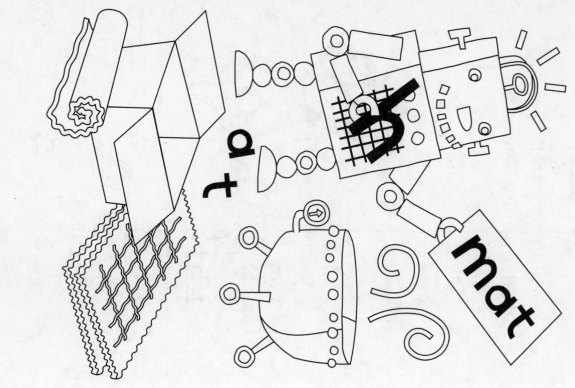

hat

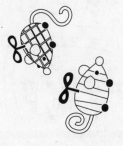

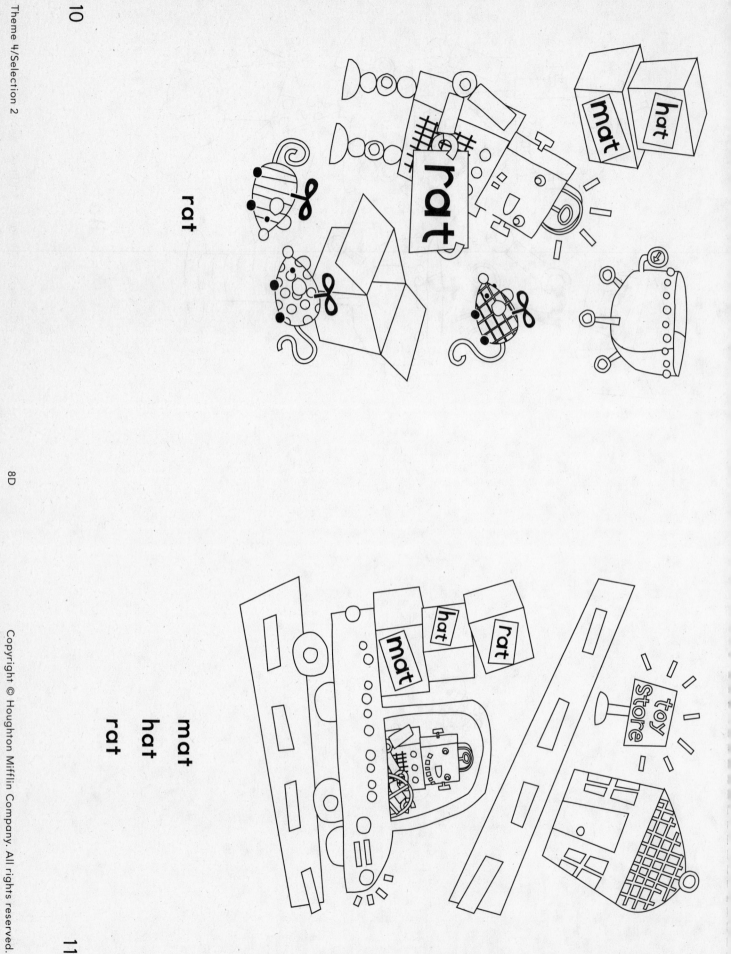

rat

mat
hat
rat

Cat Sat

by Elizabeth Kiley

illustrated by Shari Halpern

See my cat.

cat mat

Theme 4/Selection 3

cat hat
cat bat

My cat sat.
Cat!

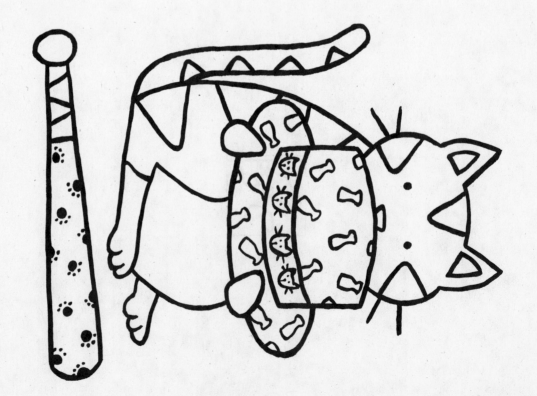

HOUGHTON MIFFLIN
Reading
A Legacy of Literacy

Let's
Count!

Nat, Pat, and Nan

by Elizabeth Kiley

illustrated by Fahimeh Amiri

1

1E

Nat sat.

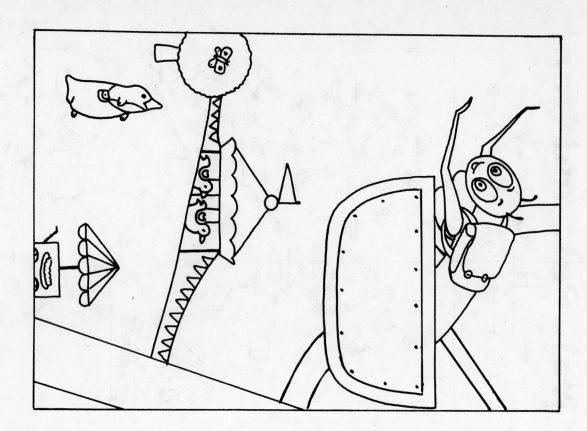

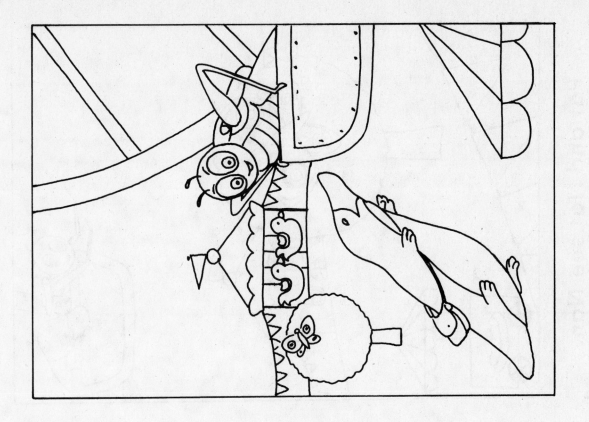

Pat ran.

Theme 5/Selection 1

4

Theme 5/Selection 1

Pat and Nat see Nan.

Nan! Nan!

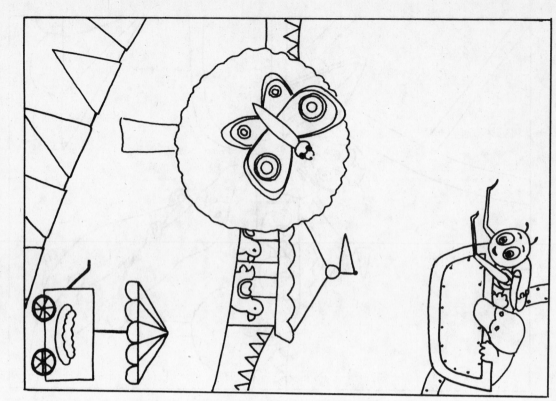

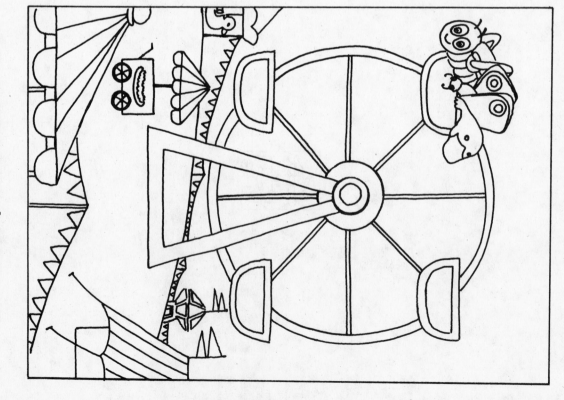

Pat, Nat, and Nan sat.

Go, Cat!

by Elizabeth Kiley

illustrated by Nancy Speir

Go, Nan!

Nan ran, ran, ran.

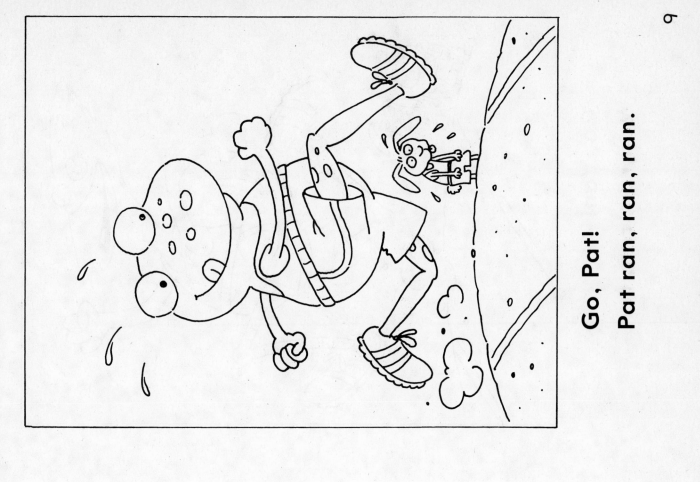

Go, Pat!

Pat ran, ran, ran.

Theme 5/Selection 2

Theme 5/Selection 2

Go, Van!
Van ran, ran, ran.

Go, Cat!
Cat sat, sat, sat.

Pat and Nan

by Elizabeth Kiley

illustrated by Penny Carter

13

14

Pat sat.

Nan ran, ran, ran.

Nan sat.

Pat ran, ran, ran.

11E

Theme 5/Selection 3

A fan!
A fan!

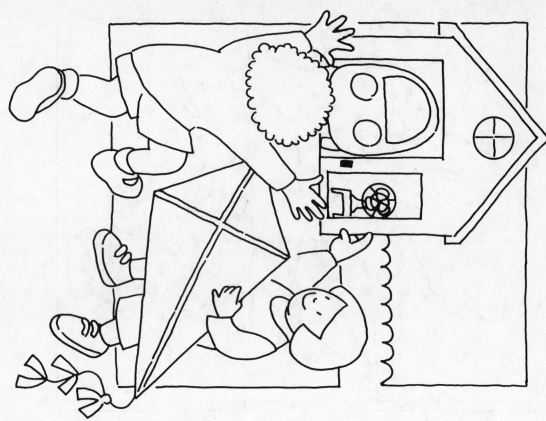

12E

Go, !

HOUGHTON MIFFLIN
Reading
A Legacy of Literacy

Sunshine and Raindrops

Can It Fit?

by Amy Griffin

illustrated by Mike Gordon

It is my van.
I can sit.

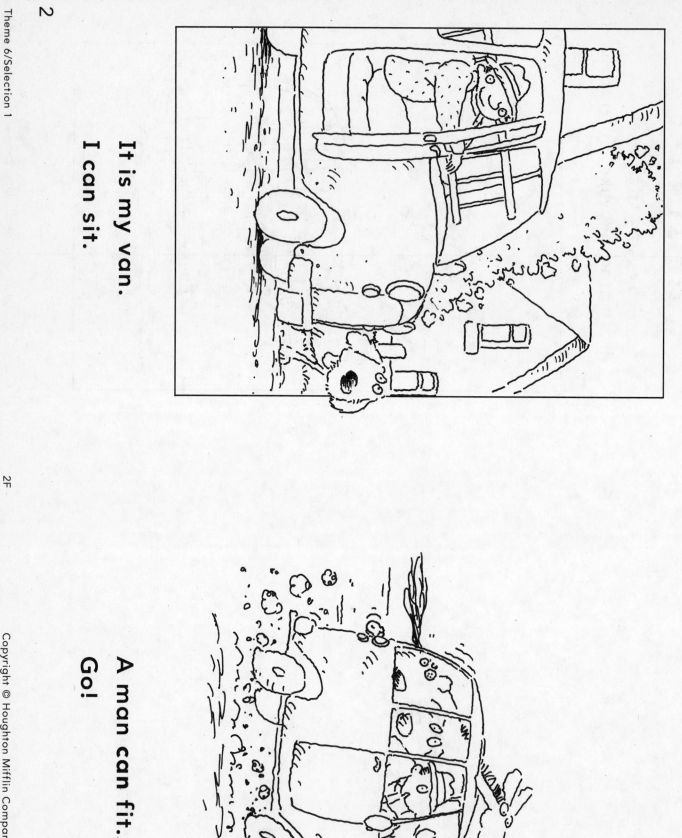

A man can fit.
Go!

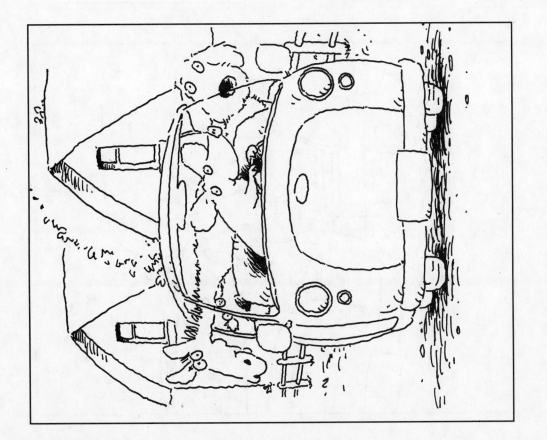

 can fit.

, sit!

Can a man fit?

Can a man sit?

Theme 6/Selection 1

Theme 6/Selection 1

Sit,  , sit!

can fit.

Sit, can fit.

, sit!

Kit

by Amy Griffin

illustrated by Alexandra Tien

9

A hat can fit Kit.

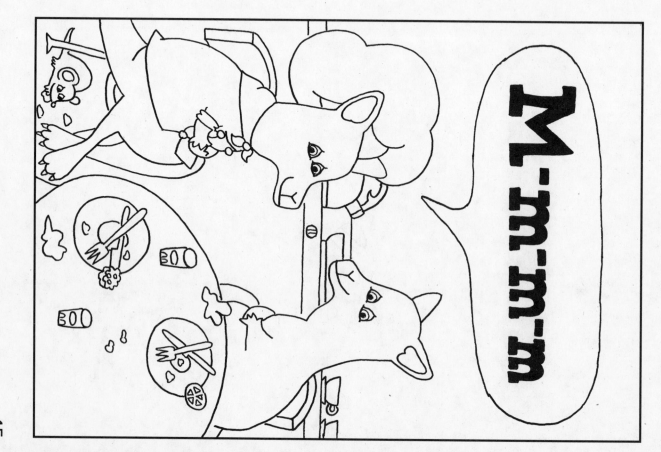

A pan can fit.

7F

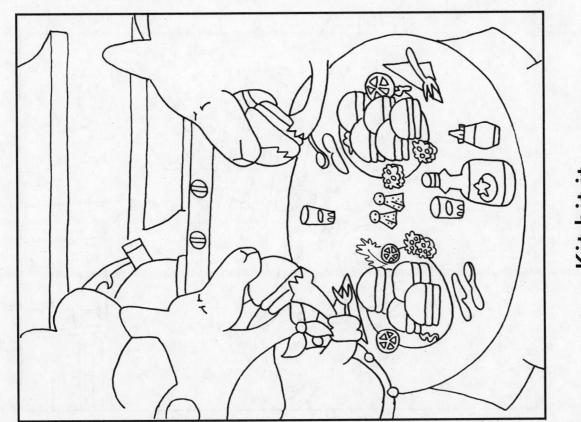

Kit bit it.
I bit it.

Theme 6/Selection 2

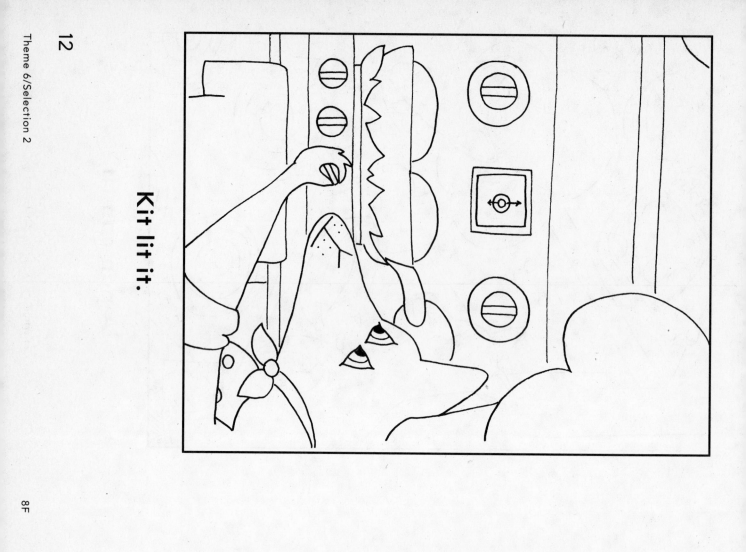

Kit lit it.

Kit can sit here.
I can sit.

Fan

by Amy Griffin

illustrated by Dagmar Fehlau

Theme 6/Selection 3

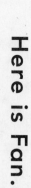

Here is Fan.

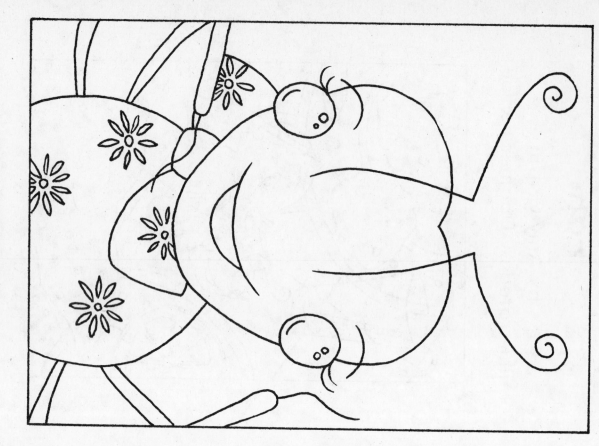

10F

Fan quit!

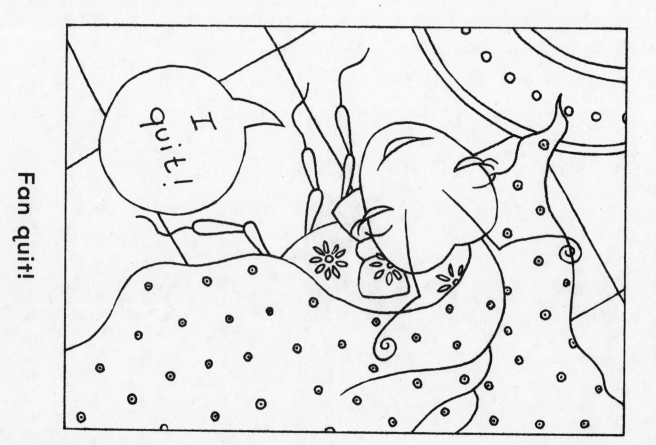

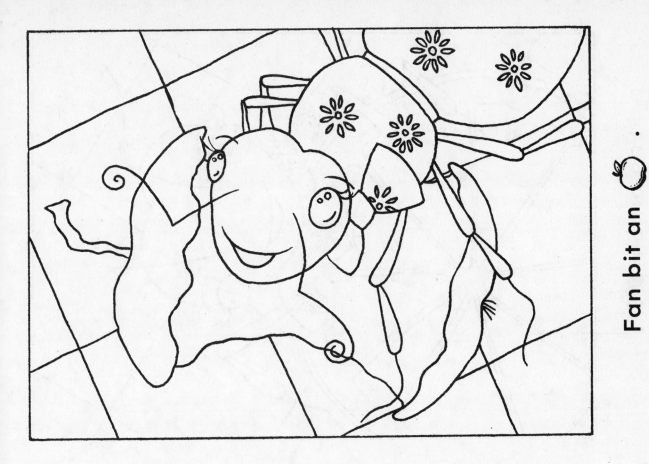

Fan bit an 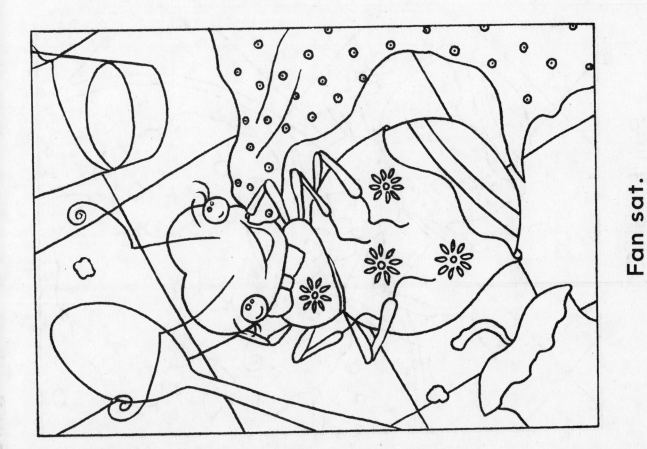.

11F

Fan sat.

Theme 6/Selection 3

Theme 6/Selection 3

Fan bit an 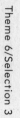 .

12F

Fan bit a 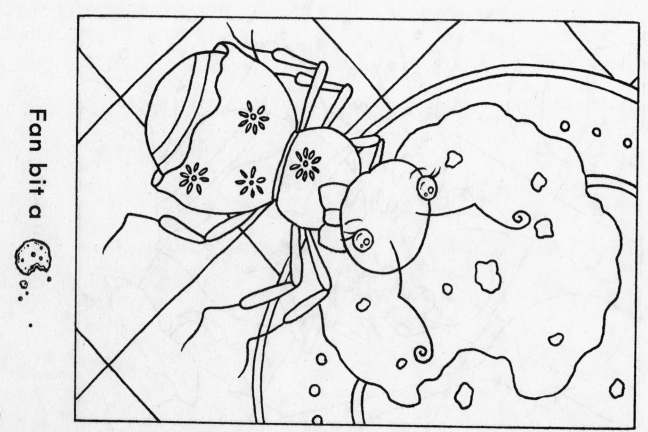 .

21

HOUGHTON MIFFLIN
Reading
A Legacy of Literacy

Wheels Go Around

Big Rig

by Amy Griffin

illustrated by Bob Kolar

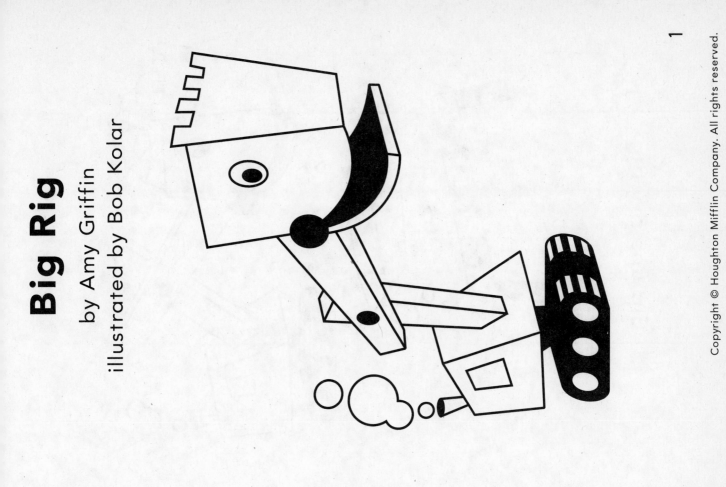

Big Rig can dig.

Dan can

Big Rig can dig.

Theme 7/Selection 1

2G

Dig, dig, dig.

3

Dan can [illustration].

3G

6

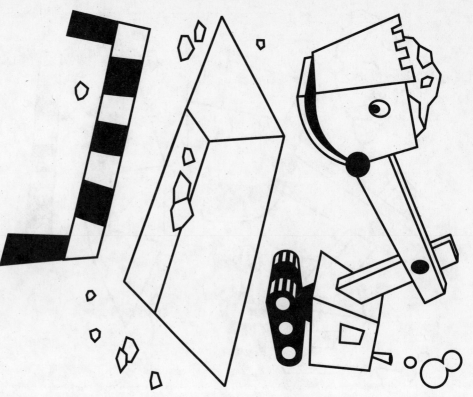

Big Rig can dig a pit.

Big Rig can dig a pit
for Dan.

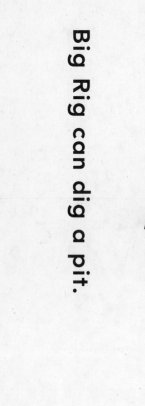

Tan Van

by Amy Griffin

illustrated by Amiko Hirao

It is a tan van!

Zig Pig ran.
Can I have it?

7G

Theme 7/Selection 2

Dan Cat ran.
Can I have it?

8G

Zig Pig sat.
Dan Cat sat.

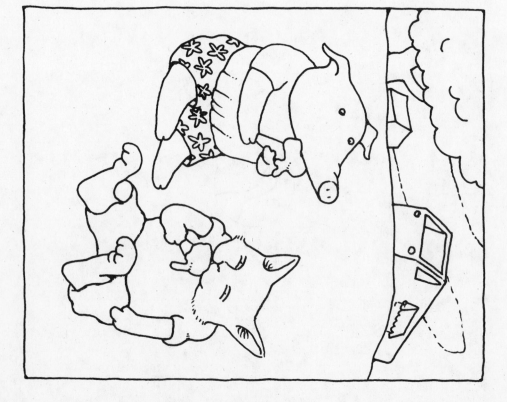

Zig Pig and Dan Cat

by Amy Griffin

illustrated by Amiko Hirao

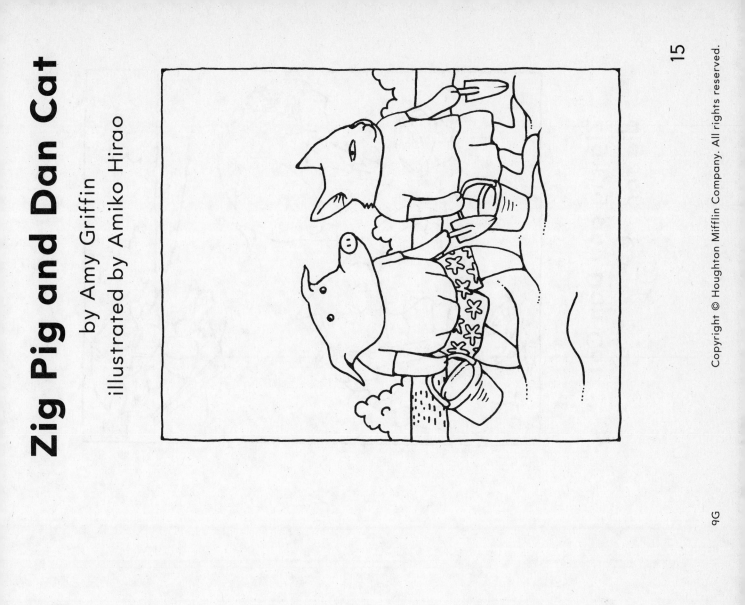

9G

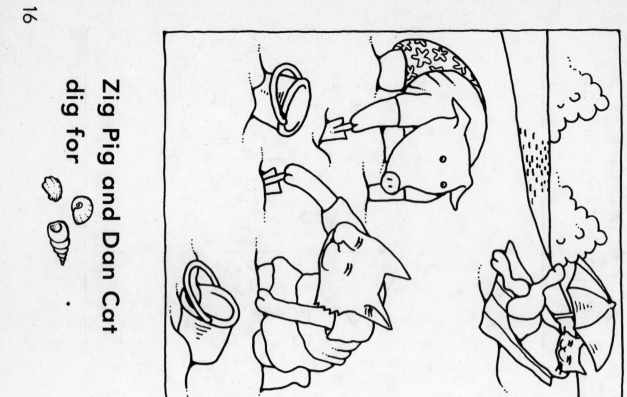

Zig Pig and Dan Cat
dig for .

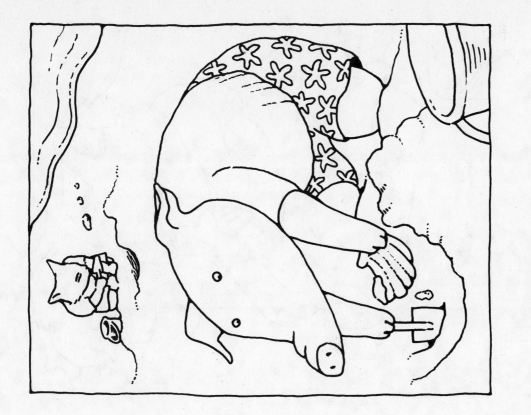

Zig Pig can dig.
I have it!

11G

Dan Cat can dig.
Here it is!

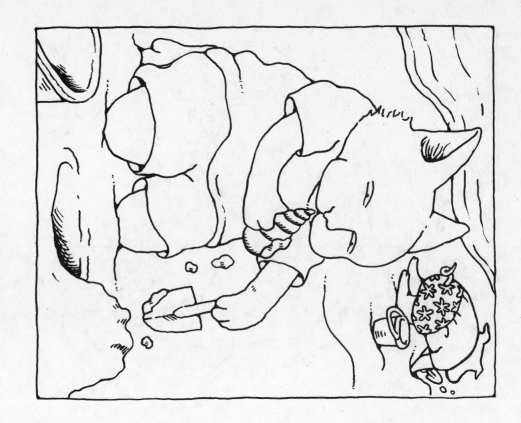

Zig Pig sat.
Dan Cat sat.

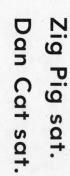

12G

HOUGHTON MIFFLIN
Reading
A Legacy of Literacy

Down on the Farm

Dot Got a Big Pot

by Ann Spivey

illustrated by Ashley Wolff

2

Dot got a big, big, big pot.

Dot got  .

Dot sat.

Nan sat.

Nat sat.

7

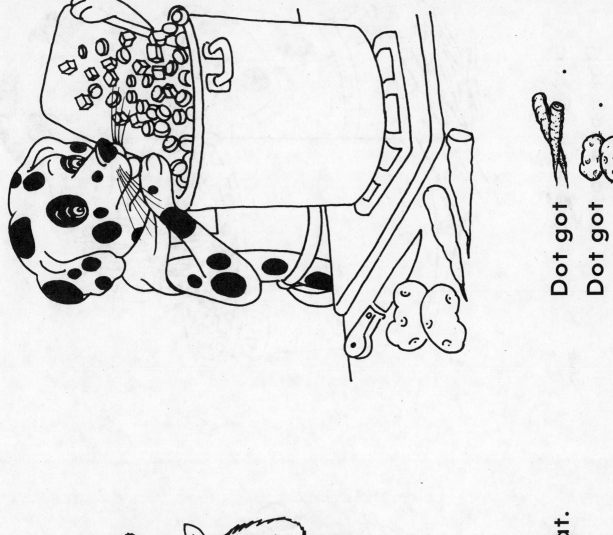

Dot got .

Dot got .

3

3H

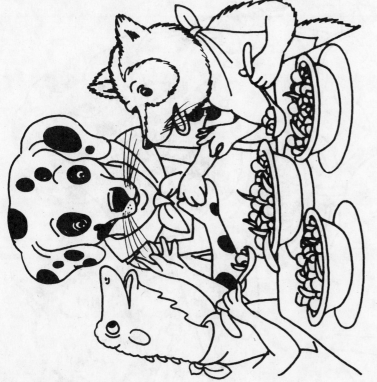

"It is hot, hot, hot!" said Nan.

"I like it hot, hot, hot!" said Nat.

6

Theme 8/Selection 1

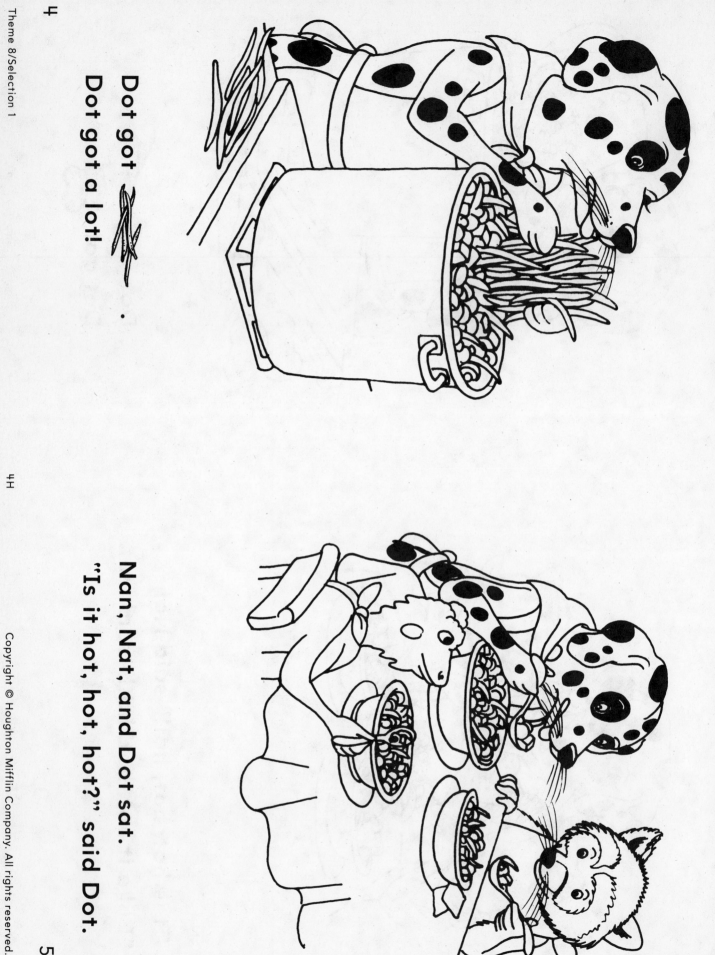

Dot got 🌾 .
Dot got a lot!

Nan, Nat, and Dot sat.
"Is it hot, hot, hot?" said Dot.

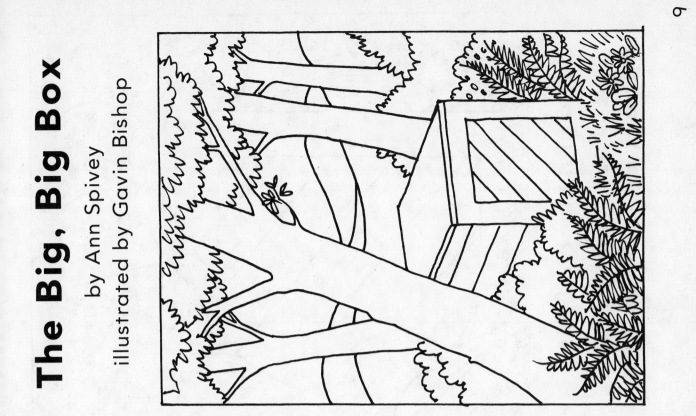

The Big, Big Box

by Ann Spivey

illustrated by Gavin Bishop

10

Theme 8/Selection 2

It is a big, big, big, big box!
"It is my big, big, big box,"
said Fan Fox.

6H

Fan sat.
Dan sat.

"It is not," said Dan Cat.
"It is my big, big, big box!"

7H

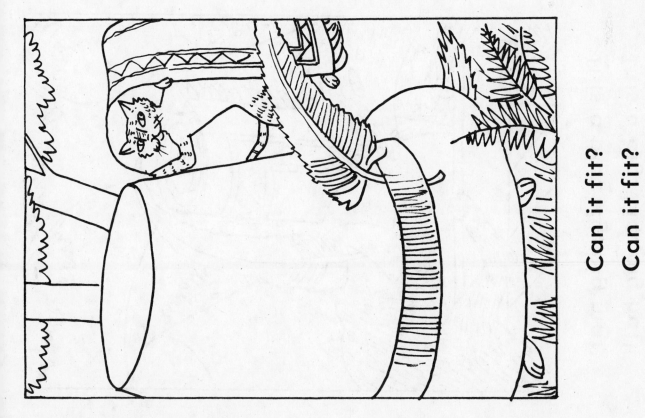

Can it fit?
Can it fit?

Theme 8/Selection 2

12

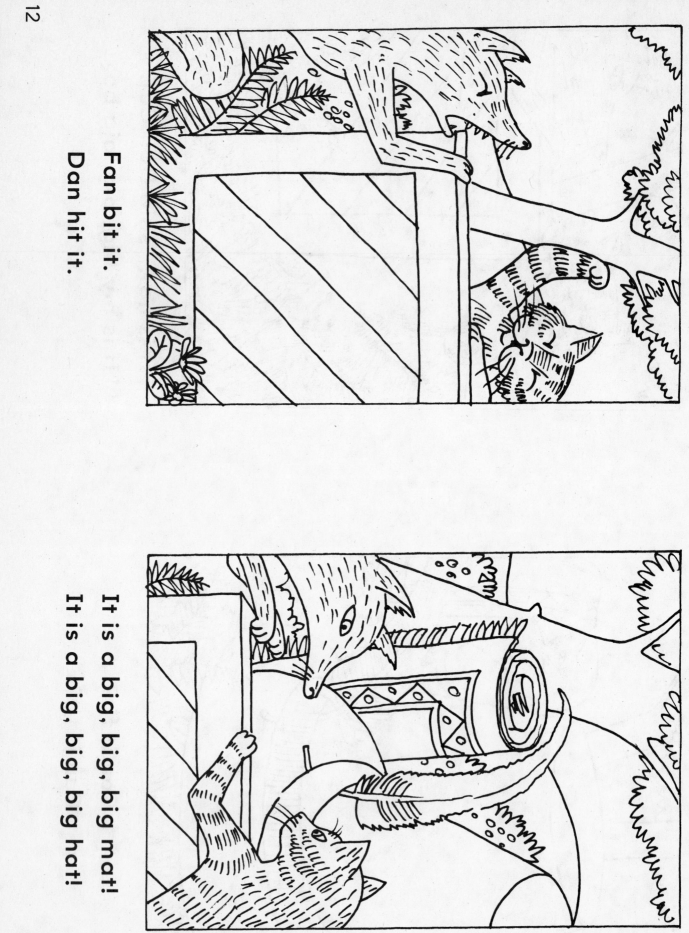

Fan bit it.
Dan hit it.

It is a big, big, big mat!
It is a big, big, big hat!

13

A Pot for Dan Cat

by Ann Spivey

illustrated by Gavin Bishop

"I can see Dan Cat,"
said Fan Fox.

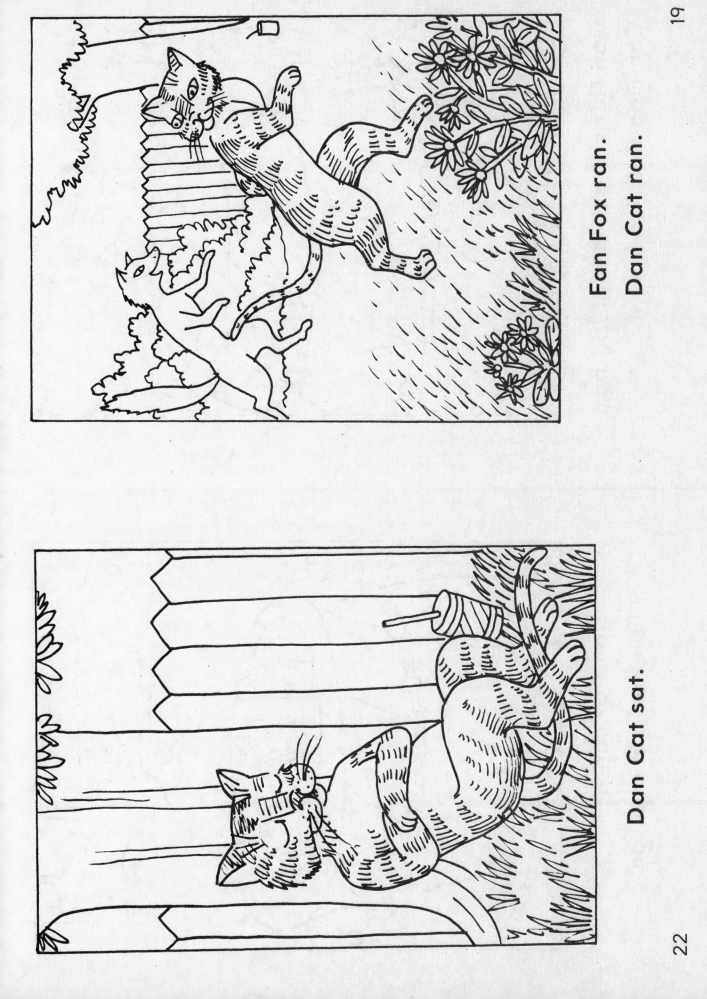

Fan Fox ran.
Dan Cat ran.

Dan Cat sat.

11H

22

Theme 8/Selection 3

Dan Cat can see a big, big, big pot.
Can Dan Cat fit?

Dan Cat can fit!
Fan Fox ran and ran.

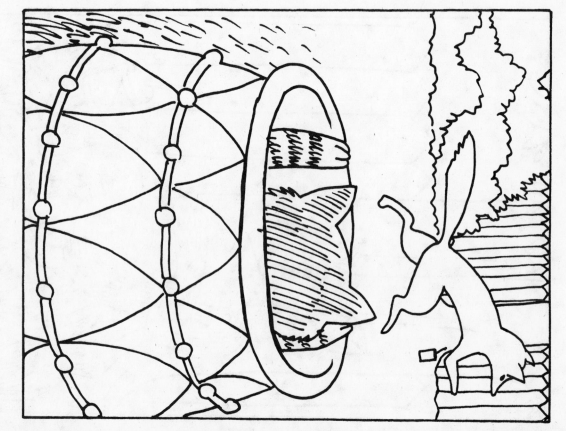

HOUGHTON MIFFLIN
Reading
A Legacy of Literacy

Spring Is Here

Get Set! Play!

by Ann Spivey

illustrated by Darcia Labrosse

2

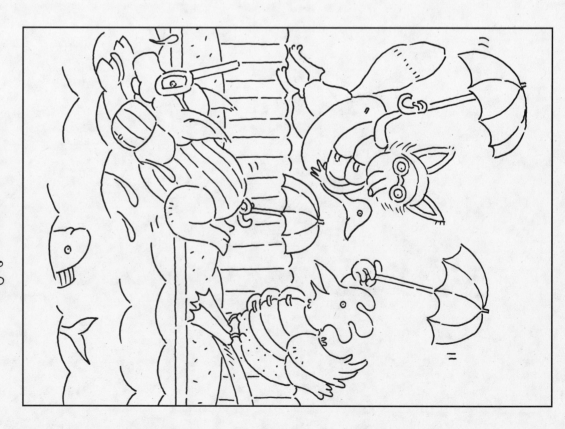

🐦 can get wet.
"Not I," said 🐦

21

Fox got 3 🐑 .
Get set! Play!

2 7

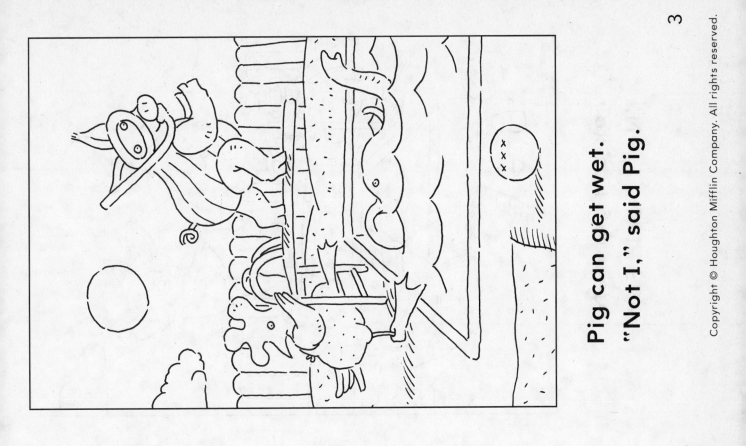

Pig can get wet.
"Not I," said Pig.

3

Pig got ___ .

6

Theme 9/Selection 1

Fox can get wet.
"Not I," said Fox.

got a .

Ben

by Ann Spivey
illustrated by Susan Calitri

Theme 9/Selection 2

"My pet!" said Ben.
"I can not get it."

Ten men got it.
Ben can play.

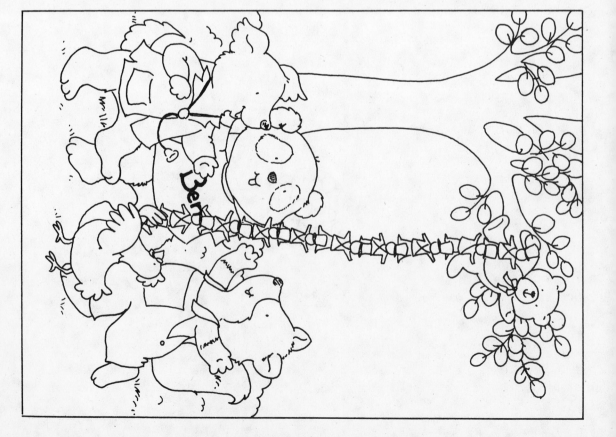

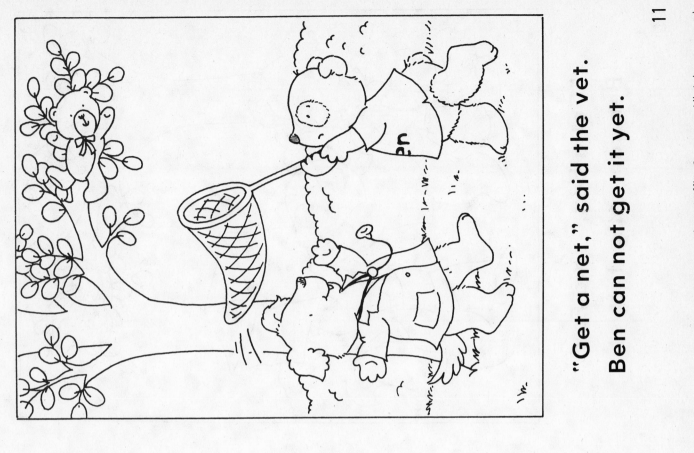

"Get a net," said the vet.

Ben can not get it yet.

71

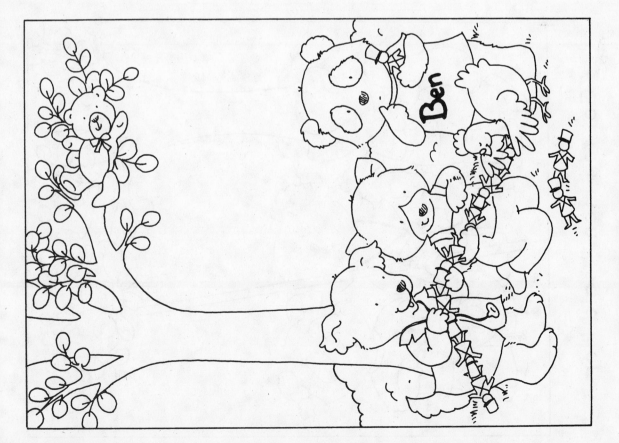

Ben got ten men.

14

"Get a box," said Fox.
Ben can not get it yet.

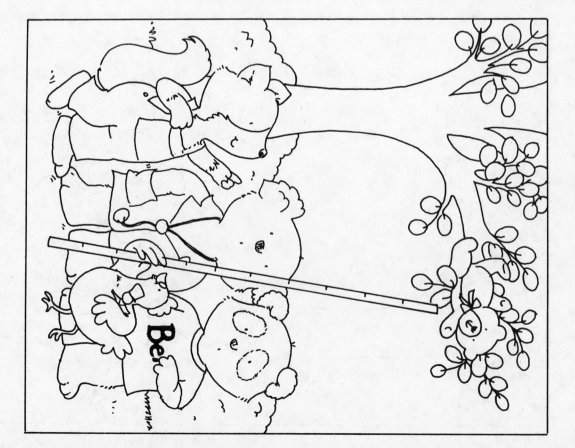

"Get ten men," said Hen.

12

13

81

Pig Can Get Wet

by Ann Spivey

illustrated by Vincent Andriani

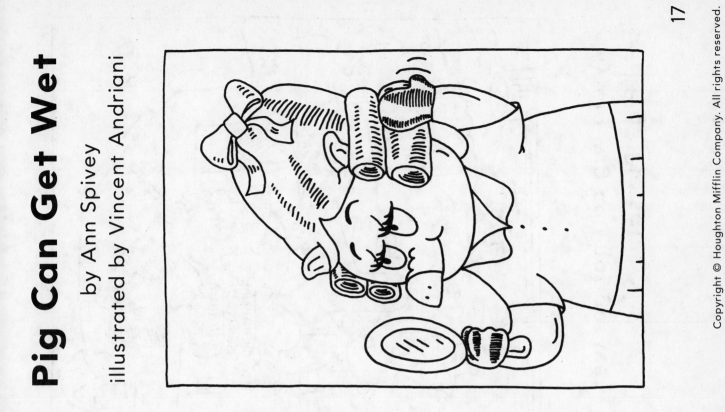

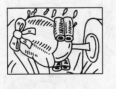

17

18

Theme 9/Selection 3

"My big wig can not get wet,"
said Pig. Pig sat.

"My big wig can not get wet."
Cat sat.

19

"A pig can get wet," she said.
"A pig can play."

22

Theme 9/Selection 3

20

Cat can sit. Pig can sit.
A big 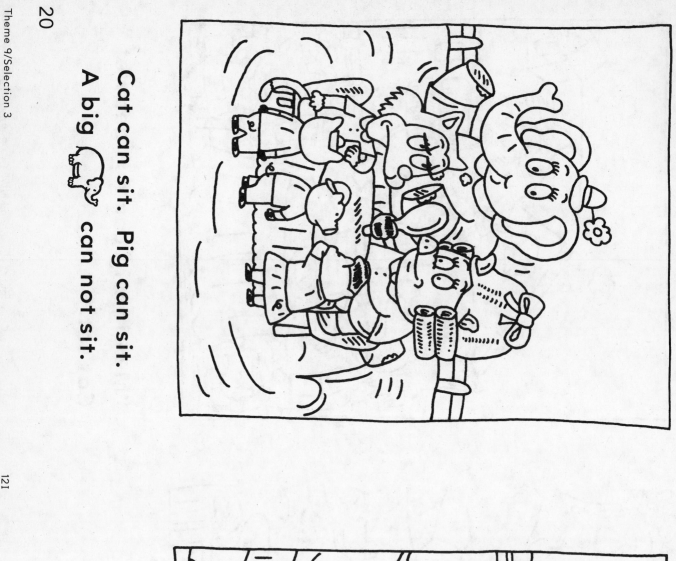 can not sit.

Cat got wet.
Pig got wet.

21

HOUGHTON MIFFLIN
Reading
A Legacy of Literacy

A World of Animals

Ken and Jen

by Thomas Alexander
illustrated by Thierry Courtin

Ken dug a big pit.

Dig, Ken, dig.

Ken and Jen are wet.

Jen dug a big pit.
Dig, Jen, dig.

 is wet.

3J

Theme 10/Selection 1

Ken dug.

Jen dug.

4

It is hot, hot, hot!

5

It Can Fit

by Thomas Alexander
illustrated by Bernadette Pons

Theme 10/Selection 2

See a big van!

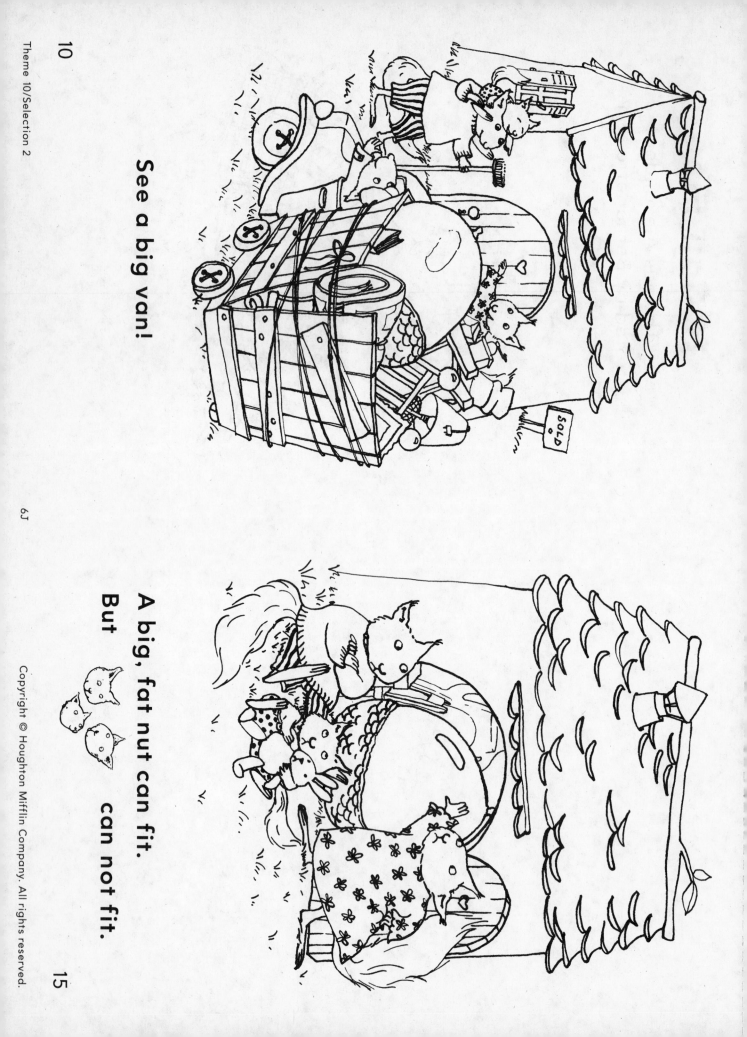

A big, fat nut can fit.
But can not fit.

6J

He can lug a big jug.
It can fit.

7J

But can a big, fat nut fit?

14

Theme 10/Selection 2

Theme 10/Selection 2

She can lug a tan rug.
It can fit.

8J

He can lug a hat box.
It can fit.

The Bug Hut

by Thomas Alexander

illustrated by Vincent Andriani

Big Bug can lug a fat box.

She CAN jig!
Jan Bug can jig, jig, jig.

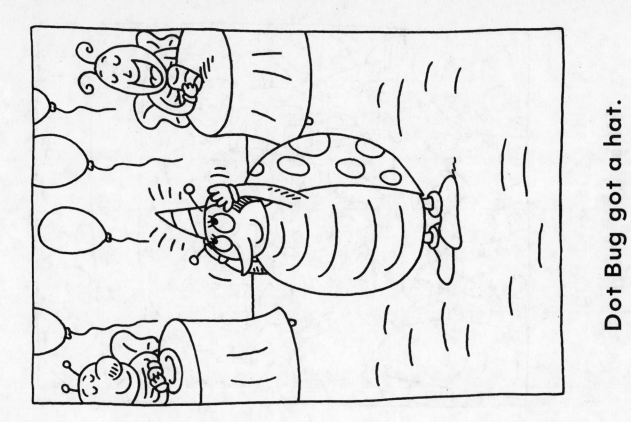

Dot Bug got a hat.

Sniff
sniff

But Jan Bug can not jig.

22

Theme 10/Selection 3

11J

Here is Jan Bug.

Hug, hug, hug!

Big Bug can jig.

Dot Bug can jig.